SOUL MESSAGES

LAVISH LOVE NOTES FOR THE SOUL

PHYLLIS CAPANNA, M.A., OTR/L

Published in 2014 by Phyllis Capanna

Printed in the United States of America

Published by phyllomania/Phyllis Capanna

Copyright © 2014 by Phyllis Capanna

All rights reserved. This book may not be reproduced or distributed for any purpose whatsoever without the express written permission of the author except for the use of brief quotations in a book review. For written permission, contact the author at the web address below. Additional copies and other formats may be ordered directly from the author at the website address below.

Soul Message Cards decks can be ordered from the author.

The material in this book is for entertainment purposes only. It is not intended to replace medical care, health care, or psychotherapy.

Cover photograph: Phyllis Capanna www.phylliscapanna.com.

Cover design and printing by CreateSpace.

ISBN: 978-0615952451

Contents

Acknowledgements	ix
How to Use the Soul Messages Cards	viii
Introduction to the Soul Messages	iv
Soul Messages	10
Where to Go From Here	61

Introduction to the Soul Messages

"You're just like…."

"You'll never…."

"You'd be so pretty/handsome/strong/popular if…."

"Nobody likes a …."

"The world doesn't…."

"He who hesitates…."

"The early bird…."

From the moment we are born, we receive messages about ourselves and about life. I received them, you received them. After decades of doing the work to heal some of my deepest-seated issues, I found I was still unhappy. At one point I looked around at my life and realized there was nothing on the outside that was really that terrible. All the suffering and drama were happening on the inside, in my thoughts, and, by extension, in my feelings.

I began to examine those thoughts and to question the worldview they expressed. I began to experiment with rejecting them. I did this in several ways. I tried to put the belief into words and then state its opposite. All of its opposites. "You're just like your father" became "You're nothing like your father" and "You're not just like your father" and "You're just like…Marlene Dietrich…Katherine Hepburn…Winston Churchill….!" I began to then see that I am my own person, unique and separate from anyone else.

Then I experimented with making other statements about myself, ones that I would love to be true but nobody, including me, had ever said about me. I went overboard and over the top, because that's who I am, and because I wanted to create a counterweight to those other statements that felt as substantial on the other end of the spectrum. "You're the most beautiful person I have ever met." "You are brilliant." "You are in exactly the right place."

If you've ever experimented with words and statements, then you have probably experienced what I have–that inside, certain words and sentiments feel really good, and certain ones don't. That's what I began to use as my measurement of whether the words were strong enough antidotes to what I had come to regard as the poisonous thoughts I was thinking. I didn't ask if they were true, I just asked my little wounded soul if they *felt* true.

With these rewording adventures and the many that followed, I began to have a space within where I could just be. I started to be curious about who I really am, something that I had never done before. I believe that in my case, no adult had really seen me and been curious to discover the uniqueness of that little person.

I began to appreciate the roots of my own suffering. To not be seen as a unique person with unique qualities–including faults– is, in a core way, not to exist. It's a short step from not existing to not having legitimate needs and feelings, and to not be fully in your own life. These were the deepest roots of my addiction and my subsequent unhappiness, even after I had successfully arrested the addictive behaviors that were causing me so much trouble.

Slowly, those habitual and ingrained beliefs and thoughts began to lose their grip on my internal environment. I began to question every thought that contained a gross generalization, because that is how to recognize a belief.

"Everyone always…."

"Nobody ever…."

"The world doesn't…."

"There's only so much _____ to go around…."

"Hurry up or you'll never…."

I began to wonder then about the whole worldview that these beliefs create. I began to question that worldview, like a close friend of mine, who, after successfully completing a fire walk, asked, "What else have I been told that is not true?"

When I created the Soul Message cards, I was developing a workshop about manifesting a dream. I knew that at the core of every failed attempt at happiness is a deep soul wound that exists because we have not been given permission to exist, to desire, to have, to enjoy, to trust. We are afraid to want, to strive, to expand, to make noise, and to be sloppy. We have believed in lack and limitation on the one hand and attaining perfection and beating others out for the prize on the other.

It's not that these conditions don't really exist or are bad. It's that they don't exist on the soul level. They exist out here in the three-dimensional world. And here's why that matters: If we believe we are limited on the soul level, as beings, we will be prohibitively limited in some area of our worldly life–either in intimacy, our financial affairs, in our career, our faith, or simply in our ability to be happy.

In the workshop, I wanted to address these soul wounds without opening them up. I wanted to invite into the circle those disenfranchised and insecure parts of ourselves and find a way to give them new messages about who they are and how the world works. I wanted to give them hope, so that the beautiful, earnest, souls in that room could actually create those shining, lovely dreams.

I wrote down every over-the-top, positive, affirming, loving, hopeful, supportive, beautiful message I could think of about our souls and about a loving Universe (which I capitalize because it helps me to think of it as a living being), decorated them a little, cut them into little cards, put them in a bowl, and brought them out at the end, during our closing.

Each participant made a quick drawing of her Inner Lost Soul. At the appropriate moment, each one welcomed that inner hurt part to the circle and read it a Soul Message. I suggested they say something like, "Little Lost Soul, welcome to this circle. I want you to know that..." and then read the message aloud.

Instantly, the atmosphere in the circle turned soft and sweet, as one by one those lost parts received welcoming, affirming messages that just happened to be perfect for the person receiving it.

Tears and smiles coexisted on broken, hopeful faces.

I want you to know that "Your beauty is an inspiration to others."

I want you to know that "It is now safe to occupy space and breathe."

I want you to know that "It is safe to share yourself with others. You matter."

It wasn't until I saw the messages in action that I realized how powerful a healing tool this deck is. As I worked with the cards, I became more and more convinced that if each of us had received these kinds of messages about ourselves and about the world–loving, kind, affirming, welcoming messages that create a sense of sanctity and hope, that foster self-confidence and encourage us to listen to our own guts–it would be a very different world. It would be the kind of world I see is possible, a world that many people sincerely want and are working toward manifesting.

Each of us needs to hear these messages as we actively work on a deep level to heal the core wounds that are holding us back from realizing our full potential.

Phyllis Capanna
March 2014
Revised August 2015

How to Use the Soul Message Cards

The Soul Message cards can be used as an oracle, picking a card at random after formulating a question. Questions like, "What belief is holding me back?" or "What does my soul most need to know?" are good ones to start with. Any time there is struggle or a situation that is eluding resolution is a good time to pick a card and ask, "What message will help me resolve or heal this?" Or you can simply sit quietly and ask for a message from Whatever you believe in, to help you in the way that you need right now.

Once you have read the message, ask yourself what might be the belief that the Soul Message is an antidote to? How does this play out in your life? What possibilities does this message open up for you?

Some people pick a card as part of their daily grounding or spiritual practice. Some work with a card a week and keep looking for where those beliefs show up as they go about their lives. Although this book is intended as a companion to the deck of Soul Message cards, it can easily be used without the cards in hand. Simply let your hand, eye, gut, or chance pick a page for you.

Hold the message lightly, keeping what resonates and laying down the rest. It is possible that a Soul Message will touch you deeply and set off a healing chain reaction, which can look like anything from instant liberation to tears and laughter, and many things between and beyond.

May you receive the messages with the utmost compassion for yourself. Wherever you are on your healing journey, I offer the Soul Messages as lavish love notes from a loving Universe to you. May these and many other tools and gifts reach you at just the right time and help you create the wonderful life you deserve.

Acknowledgments

This book would not have been possible were it not for a conspiracy of circumstances that enabled me to sit down at the empty page with my fountain pen and write until I was done. I believe I have the loving Universe to thank for that.

In addition, several humans have been my cheerleading, encouraging, sustenance, and creative cauldron squad for years, and they deserve some recognition in print.

Deb Gowen, the sister my parents didn't have, has supported every single crazy thing I have done. Over the years our friendship has become the go-to place for the reality check I usually cannot give myself. She is why I believe everything I need I already have.

Eileen Mielenhausen, creative imp, goddess of the event, and adventuresome collaborator, has provided me with countless opportunities to create, facilitate, improvise, and enjoy women's gatherings and workshops in beautiful places in our chosen home state of Maine, including the workshop that spawned the Soul Messages.

My partner Robyn Deveney has the patience of a saint, the calm of the Buddha, and a healing touch like none other. She knows when to let me rant and when to talk back (an option not for wimps.) Most of all, she gives me tons of Sagittarian space in which to pursue my creative callings. Her support and love are my anchors.

Last but not least, the many women and men–clients, workshop participants, advisers, advisees, and friends–who have shared their hearts and souls in this amazing dance of self-discovery and expansion, have been models of courageous vulnerability and healing.

On your spirits have I built my faith.
Thank you for your love.

SOUL MESSAGES

LAVISH LOVE NOTES FOR THE SOUL

> **BE SEEN. YOU ARE SAFE. THE UNIVERSE ADORES YOU.**

This message comes at a time when you could blossom. It is up to you to allow that to happen. Knowing it is possible is a good first step. But perhaps it is time for second, third, and fourth steps. Maybe you are stopping yourself for fear of being seen and not measuring up.

Just showing up takes courage, doesn't it?

It may be that you have developed ways of hiding in an effort to protect yourself from harm, judgment, or ridicule. What are your favorite ways of hiding? Do you keep silent when you feel like speaking? Do you conform to avoid attention? Are you afraid that if you let the people around you see you as being unique and separate from them–and maybe not who they need you to be–you will be less loved, less connected, less than?

The Universe wants you to know you are capable of protecting your boundaries without hiding. This is a big step. It involves believing in yourself enough to take some chances. It's okay–in fact, recommended–to start small and work up from there. With each step you gain confidence. Ask yourself, "When do I hide? What do I stop myself from doing? How am I not supposed to be?"

The Universe adores you. And, you can presume, is somewhere, clapping, pointing, smiling, and saying, "That's Mine! I made that one! Isn't she magnificent?" This is the love you need to picture when you consider putting yourself out there a little more visibly.

This same loving Universe wants you to know that now is the time to grow out of self-imposed limits, and when you do, you will be pleasantly surprised at the rewards.

> **Breathe in the loving Universe.
> It is all around you.**

If you have been feeling unsafe or disconnected from your spirit, this message has come to remind you that you are living in a loving Universe that is as close as your next breath.

There are two important points here. The first is the reminder to stop and breathe. Perhaps you have been a little tense, or intense, and have left your body behind. Take some nice deep breaths (ten is a good number) and get back into your body. Don't rush this. Allow all of you to catch up.

Second, the Universe is a loving place. There is love for you, specifically. Think of yourself as swimming in a sea of love. Let it in through your pores. You need to remember that Life Force is love, is creation and creative. It is your home, your element, your energy, and your fuel.

Relax into a loving Universe. Rest in the loving Universe. Talk and listen to the loving Universe. Allow It to nurture you. Notice the grand conspiracy of nurturing and sustenance there is for you–light, air, water, food, color, taste, friends, snow, etc.

This life is all about life! Being alive is what this trip is about.

Stop and breathe in the life-giving fuels, especially the soul-feeding love that is all around you.

Delight yourself.

The Universe wants you to know that no one else can delight you as well as you can. You may feel you have no idea how. It is time to learn. Look and listen for tiny, tentative, but unmistakable yearnings, preferences, and curiosities. The good news is, because you are so fun deficient, delighting yourself is actually easy. But you have to stop long enough to listen to what your heart and soul are craving.

This message comes to you at a time when you are being too hard on yourself. You have decided that what is good for you are things like discipline, commitment, hard work, and structure. This may be true for part of you. Your heart, though, is starving for beauty and lightness, enjoyment and fun. Consider that a delighted you is a powerful and creative you. Know that lightness and laughter are the perfect healers for you right now.

Not all productivity and accomplishment come from focusing on self-improvement. Not all worthy achievements are attained through hard work. To-do lists are not the quickest way to happiness. There is something to be said for productive downtime that allows your being to integrate the lessons recently learned. Often a period of relaxed discipline yields a new normal, one that solidifies new skills and knowledge into a better functioning whole.

The Universe loves you and wants you to be happy. And so do all your loved ones. It is only you standing in the way. Go for it! You may have been uttering the words, "I can't" and "not now" a lot lately. It is time you stopped carrying on the grimness campaign started in your childhood.

You deserve to be delighted, daily!

Everything you need to fulfill your dreams is here for you.

In other words, the pieces are in place. Not some of them someday, but all of them, now. It's up to you to take actions that will allow them to come together for you.

The best steps to take are the most obvious ones. Not sure what's right in front of you? Try asking for what you need. Need a studio or office space? Ask. Knock on doors, fill out applications, talk to resource people. Ask, "Who could help me with this?" Get together with a friend and brainstorm. Practice listening with an open mind for what's possible instead of focusing on what seems impossible.

Out of fear, you have not taken the steps that you can take. By actively engaging in making it happen, you create energy around your dream. And here's the trick: Don't get hung up on immediate results. Just take actions. Trust your instincts.

Picture yourself and your daily world. Now picture a door right there in the room with you. On the other side of that door is your dream, come true. In your imagination, open that door and step into your dream. Feel what it feels like to have it, real, in your life. Yippee! It's great, isn't it?

This message is about opening that door. What is in the way of receiving your good? Hint: It isn't circumstances or other people. What do you believe about your Universal birthright of good? And what do you believe about your dream? Is it possible? Do you deserve it? Are you worthy, yet?

In this creative partnership, the Universe is saying it is your turn to take the lead, and the Universe will yield it all to you.

> **FALL INTO THE ARMS OF THE UNIVERSE AND ALLOW YOURSELF TO BE CARRIED.**

Sometimes you need to be reminded that there is something Greater afoot, Something more powerful than you that is orchestrating life.

Now is one of those times.

Even if you think you are working in concert with the Universe, take a moment to check in on how loosely you are holding the outcome, and how much effort you are using to keep things on track.

You may feel you need to work hard right now, and that is okay. Remember that even though you may need to employ a certain amount of tension to stay afloat, you *are* being carried by a great current.

But assuming you are not literally being swept away, you can afford to take at least a restful few moments and allow yourself to be supported, if only by a cushion and a couch. While you are resting, connect with Something larger. Ask for help and continued support in your endeavors.

You may have developed a belief and coping strategy that says you are in this alone. The Universe is inviting you to partner with it, encouraging you to cross some tasks off your list and give them to the Universe to take care of.

Above all, know that no matter what the outcome, you will be okay.

IT IS NOW SAFE TO EXPAND INTO YOUR HIGHEST POTENTIAL.

It is no longer necessary to shrink yourself down to a size that is comfortable for somebody else, past or present–not your ideas, beliefs, goals, colors, voice, actions, or projects. Not only it is safe to become more fully yourself, it is in fact preferable, inevitable, and strongly wants to happen. Furthermore, your highest potential is a lot bigger than you know.

Does it feel like Universal Wisdom is conspiring to have you grow right now? You may be getting challenging situations and finding that you can handle them. You may also be finding that supportive people, time and space to process, intuitive flashes, good instincts, and opportunities are coming your way with more frequency.

What if anything do you fear in becoming bigger than you thought it safe to be? What do you hope? How will you cooperate with the energies of growth and expansion? What is your favorite way of resisting?

Whatever your answers to these questions, now is a time to make sure you are acting in cooperation with the energies of expansion and highest good.

Staying small out of habit was a useful adaptation at some point in your life. Remember that acts of sabotage are often quiet, subtle, and rational. If you find yourself rationalizing your choices, you might want to look again. But by the same token, notice what inspires you. It may take some practice to awaken your capacity to be inspired, if you are used to staying small and playing it "safe."

> *It is now safe to occupy space and breathe.*

You are someone who on some level has believed that the world, your family, even you would be better off if you were not around. You have developed physical and energetic strategies to take up as little space as possible. You are uncomfortable when people do things for you. You avoid attention. You try not to take too much of anyone's time. You may have kept yourself small physically. People startle when you speak, because they didn't know you were standing there, and because you don't speak up often. The fewer waves you make, you decided, the better.

Until now. The Universe wants you to know that you have taken this strategy as far as it can go. It worked and was necessary in the past, and now it is time to allow yourself to be here. Take up space, breathe, make noise, have needs, claim your share.

You will have to get used to hearing the sound of your own voice. You will find yourself creating messes and calling attention to yourself, and this will feel uncomfortable, but also a little exhilarating. The truth is, it has become uncomfortable to keep up these I'm-not-really-here strategies. You want more. The good news is, it hurts more in the place you're in right now than it will in a little while when you let your breath out and decide to live this life as best you can.

On some level you are itching to roll up your sleeves and get your hands dirty. This is a good thing, because you are here, and you are needed in full. Take a deep breath and allow yourself to arrive fully into this moment. The threat is gone. Give yourself permission to be here, be who you are, and live your life as you desire.

> *It is now safe to receive all of life's blessings.*

Have you been feeling that the Blessing Train with all life's goodies has passed you by? Are you secretly relieved, vowing to stick with the familiar state of affairs and make do? Do you doubt your ability to handle things if they should suddenly turn good?

This message comes to you now to encourage you to open to receiving goodness, especially that certain something you have quietly decided is just not going to happen for you in this life. You feel you might crack if that possibility opens up again. You had emptied that room, swept it clean, locked all the windows, and closed that door. You even put a nice, solid bureau in front of it to convince yourself that it isn't really there.

The Universe is telling you that it is safe to let your heart open, for that is what must happen if you are to allow yourself to desire again. If you have been in a holding pattern, neither drawing nor discarding, but passing each time it's your turn, this message is telling you to play your cards. It will be okay, maybe better than okay.

Most of all, this message is about examining the mental limits you have placed on the abundance that can blossom in your life and to gently expand your idea of what is possible. You may already know it is safe to receive some of life's blessings. That way no one can accuse you of taking more than your share. Please remember your having what you need does not mean taking away from someone else.

Now you are being reminded to be willing to accept all of life's blessings. Are you willing to have that kind of life? Remember, you are deeply loved.

> **It is now safe to relax and enjoy yourself.**

The Universe wants you to know that nothing bad is going to happen if you go out and play. You don't have to stay around home taking care of things that your dysfunctional parents should be taking care of.

If you're a grown-up, this is your ticket out of becoming that dysfunctional parent–whether you have children or not!

This message means that it's time you allowed yourself to connect with relaxation and fun and to experience carefree time and safe space. Relax your vigilance. Something trustworthy is in charge.

Put yourself in a reclining position, make a plan to go swimming, digging in the garden, or walking to a yard sale. Make an appointment to do nothing but sip an iced tea. Go to a movie that no one else wants to see and enjoy eating the popcorn all by yourself. Buy a junky magazine. Pick up some watercolors.

The Universe wants you to know that whether you choose to relax into the moment or stand guard against it, this moment belongs to you, and you belong here, in life.

"I can't relax, I'm about to fall flat on my face!" some part of you may be protesting. Can you let up on yourself? Life is not a performance, but it can be a dance.

You may find yourself in an awkward, in-between place for a while, as the Universe presents you with more opportunities to choose to relax and enjoy, letting someone else clean, fix, or solve the latest mess.

Take a deep breath. You deserve to enjoy this one and only moment.

> **IT IS OK TO FAIL. THE UNIVERSE IS ON YOUR SIDE.**

Okay to fail. That's an idea you don't hear very often. How can it be okay to fail? Isn't failure the end of the world? The Universe wants you to reframe your idea of failure. It is nothing more than falling short of an ideal or not making a goal. Failing is to have something break down or misfire.

Failure is as much a part of life on Earth as when projects are completed, goals are met, and plants bear fruit. Failure is not wrong, it just is. Use the opportunity to gather more data, make adjustments, and try again.

What's more, the Universe is on your side. The Universe does not abandon you because you screw up or don't succeed at something. The Universe and its laws are eternal, unconditional, and impartial. The Universe is always giving to you.

Every time you begin anew, you have the opportunity to breathe life and energy into something you are trying to create. Every time. "Three strikes and you're out" is not Universal law. Neither is "If at first you don't succeed, try and try again." The Universe is still on your side even if after a few trials you decide to abandon a goal and go for something else.

It might be helpful to remember that the odds of a penny coming up heads are fifty-fifty, no matter how many times you toss it. You will either succeed or fail. Or, you will have a mushy goal and not quite know. Or, you will lose interest and walk away. All of these outcomes are whatever you make of them. It's not that the Universe wants to encourage you to fail. It wants to encourage you to try by helping take the sting–and fear–out of the possibility of failure.

> **IT IS OKAY TO NOT KNOW. YOU ARE GUIDED AND PROTECTED ALWAYS.**

It is a little disconcerting to discover you are walking a path and do not know where you are or where you are going. In other words, you are lost.

The Universe wants you to know that you may *feel* lost, but you are, in fact, being guided and protected. You don't actually have to know that much about the path you are walking in order to keep putting one foot in front of the other.

You were trained to believe that you are the one directing the journey, when it is the loving Universe that is making the travel plans, reserving your spot, readying the destination, and sending you what you need as you go.

Rest assured that you are still making progress, despite the apparent standstill in your outward circumstances. The most important thing to remember is to call on the protection and guidance that is there for you. Ask for help along the way. It will come in the form of ideas, resources, people, and other things you need.

Before you know it, you will wake up on a new day in a new place, and you will see without a doubt that Something was guiding you and clearing your path the whole time.

Until that time, enjoy the journey! Sit back and look out the window. Try reaching out to fellow travelers. Who knows? You just might be the one to give someone else some needed encouragement as you travel side by side.

> **IT IS SAFE TO LISTEN TO YOUR HEART.**

But your heart is all messy inside. It wants stuff that's crazy to want. Your heart is leading one way, and practicality demands another direction, right? What's that you say? You're not sure how to listen to your heart? Ah, then it must be aching with neglect and needing some attention.

Stop right now, put your hand on your heart center, and take the time to listen to what is in your heart. It is now safe to do this, because you are a safe listener and lover of your own innermost tenderness, love, desires, and caring. If you can't feel anything, ask, "What do I deeply care about? Whom do I love unconditionally? Is my heart broken?"

Some people's entire life navigation system is in their hearts! When steering with their heads, they tend to feel conflicted, unsettled, and unhappy, like they are perpetually multitasking. Others simply have a lot of feeling just waiting to be released. How to release what's there? Try writing, singing, going to a sad movie or a comedy. Take a yoga class and breathe. Look through a photo album. Take a walk and look for things that seem dear to you. The heart speaks through laughter and tears. It is passionate and juicy. Passionate, juicy? You? Yes, you. Remember that messy is not the same as unsafe. Let messy be okay.

This message wants you to know it is okay to have feelings, passion, love, and desire! Before you can know what to do with them you must listen to your heart. The best way to create safety is to keep what your heart tells you in respectful confidence, and to promise yourself you will not judge yourself for its contents. Once you can do that for yourself, you can begin to attract others who are also safe.

> **It is safe to share yourself with others. You matter.**

Of all the misguided things you tell yourself, perhaps "I don't make a difference" is the worst. It is both a devaluing of yourself and a way of evading responsibility for the impact you have on others.

Maybe you have been in a hiding/healing place after a breakup or a breakdown. You have decided to protect yourself from further hurt by keeping your cards close to your vest. Trouble is, that's no way to play a winning hand.

The trick to life is realizing that when we all show our hands, we get to pick the best of each and combine them to make something truly greater than the sum of its parts. It is time for you to know that what you've got is needed and valued by others.

You are here, and it does matter!

This message is coming to you at a time when you are ready to break out of old ways of being that kept you safe. You are ready to venture into new territory and let the people in your life know what you are all about.

You have developed the inner strength to withstand other people's opinions without crumbling. In fact, you are beginning to realize it doesn't matter what other people think.

It is time to tell people you love them and let them into your personal life. Just expressing a preference or sharing an experience from your day can open the way to greater intimacy and connection.

Other people will welcome the gift of you. And you will benefit in the exchange of good will and sense of belonging that follows.

JUST BEING YOU IS ENOUGH. YOU ARE A GIFT.

Does it feel wrong not to bring a gift when you go somewhere as a guest? This message wants you to imagine showing up with nothing but yourself. How would that feel? It is not bad to come with a hostess gift, but it is much better to do it out of love and generosity than out of a sense of making up for something that you inherently lack.

The Universe would like you to try showing up with just you, your big heart and appreciative presence. If you have been doing or giving to gain entry, know that you are the gift, when you are truly present. Do not cut yourself off from the real exchange of giving and receiving by fretting over tokens.

Think about the other people in the situation and get in touch with what's great about them. Are you looking forward to seeing them and catching up on everything that's going on with them? In other words, are you so focused on you that you have forgotten there are other people there, too?

That's the paradox of this message. Just being you is a gift, but you have to give it. In order to do that, you have to forget about yourself and focus on what you are giving yourself to. Think for a moment of the places you go without any conscious thought that your presence matters: the grocery store, a concert, a walk down the block. This message is reminding you that wherever you are, if you bring your conscious awareness to the situation and focus on the real people around you, you are bringing a precious gift.

It is time for you to know that you are enough. If you are still protesting that you give gifts because you want to, then try doing so without an occasion, anonymously, and let go of the need to do a little extra every time.

Relax into your wisdom. Your leadership is a gift.

You have been working hard on yourself. You have been self-examining and taking responsibility. Maybe you have made significant changes recently. You have had your nose to the grindstone so long that you haven't noticed just how far you have come.

You are in a place of wisdom now. Not that you will stop growing, but there has been so much clearing out of unproductive habits and outdated beliefs that you are in a place of internal congruence.

Because you have less struggle going on right now, you are better able to access your innate wisdom. It comes so naturally now that you hardly take note.

The Universe wants you to know that you are a natural leader, because you have done such intense inner work, and because you can see and empathize so deeply with what others are going through. The best leaders lead by example and live their message. You are such a one.

Your leadership is a gift to others traversing the path you have already walked. You have only to offer it, in humility and in love. Even indirectly, your inner work now benefits others.

Find quiet and loving ways to let people know that you know, and you will be gifted with the satisfaction of seeing the fruits of your labor come to bear in others' lives as well as your own. Your leadership is a gift that will give in both directions.

> **SHARE YOUR HEART. YOU LIGHT THE WAY FOR OTHERS.**

Your world is the world of the heart. You have been trying to function in the world of ideas, analysis, and logic. You have done a pretty good job of it, but you have hit a wall. It is time to speak your own heart language and share it with others. When you function in the cerebral world, it is as if you are speaking a second language. You have become accustomed to following the lead of others who are speaking their native tongue. But when you switch to your first language, the language of the heart, you are the leader, and others are waiting to hear from you.

This is a shift for you: to think of yourself as having something to say that others find worth hearing. The wisdom in our hearts is what is most disregarded and most needed at this time. Imagine a world in which decisions and choices were made from the heart. Imagine your life if you allowed yourself to live from your heart.

Share your heart, for others need to be shown that it can be done. The Universe wants you to know you are capable of a heart-centered leadership that feels consistent with who you are, and that when you allow yourself this gift, you will know a satisfaction and joy that you have not known previously.

To get in contact with heart energy, spend some quiet time contemplating love, passion, caring, poetry, beauty, music, romance, sadness or melancholy, belonging and community. Don't be afraid to feel the feelings of your homeland. You bring something that is missing for others.

SHARE YOUR VISION. YOU WILL INSPIRE SOMEONE TO SEE DIFFERENTLY.

Human beings are wired to be copycats. Being part of the group equals survival, so we tend to push aside the thoughts, ideas, beliefs, and even behaviors that we don't see reflected in others around us. We carry a deep fear of rejection, exile, and persecution. We will do anything to avoid losing our membership in the group.

There comes a time, however, when we have to risk rejection in order to be true to ourselves. Otherwise, we stop growing, stagnate, and eventually wither and die, spiritually and energetically.

The truth is, if you have outgrown your group, the only way to find your tribe is to share your real self. When you share your vision of life, you show who you are so that others on a similar path can find you. You step out of being a follower into being a leader.

And when one person expresses one of these heretofore unthought of ideas, others begin to speak up, too. This is how humanity evolves.

As you reach new places within, it is important to find ways to express yourself. In so doing, you may even help others evolve in their thinking or behavior by your example.

Rather than being thrown out or rejected, you may be surprised to find yourself being embraced and welcomed by kindred souls.

The Universe adores you.

The Universe creates by loving, as do you. The Universe holds you and listens to your heart. It pours loving, adoring, nurturing energy into and through you, as a natural expression of delight in Its creation.

The Universe has provided everything you need, physically, emotionally, mentally, and spiritually to thrive and to blossom. How far you go and what you eventually become, even the Universe does not know.

The Universe gave you potential, possibility, and promise. You supply belief, choice, and action.

Why not believe in a loving, adoring, actively-cheering-you-on Universe? Why not believe that a loving Universe sees, knows, and adores you personally, for all and everything in you, both actual and potential?

For too long, the belief that you must earn love and become worthy has colored your soul with a sense of isolation. The loving seed you carry has been disempowered by this construct. The result is that you have spent much of your life searching for something you already have.

Post this message on your mirror, dashboard, notebook cover and refrigerator! The Universe adores you.

With that as your foundation, how much more is possible?

> **THE WORLD IS BLESSED THAT YOU ARE HERE.**

Well, this is a no-brainer, but you may not be feeling this right now. You may be feeling the opposite, or you may be focused on what the world can do for you, forgetting that your presence makes a difference for others.

We take existence for granted and think that life is something that goes on with or without us. We join it in progress when we are born, and it continues after we die. But while you are here, everything about you makes a difference. Everything would be different without you.

You may not know the kind of blessing you bring, or the way in which your particular blessing manifests itself in others' lives. It might be a core energy of peace or acceptance that you embody, a gentleness or innocence of spirit, or it may be the energy of kind works or kind words. Perhaps you are sensitive to others' suffering so that they know they are not alone. You may have a weakness for lost and hurt creatures, or a quirky sense of humor. The colors you wear, your smile, your devotion, your music or poems–There is something you bring that makes it better for whomever comes in contact with you, and, by extension, the world.

Know this, breathe it into your awareness, and spend some time appreciating yourself today. If you have been focused on "what's wrong with me," this message is asking you to explore what's right. Sit down and make a list of what is right about you. By focusing your awareness on the good, you add to it. Make this a habit, and you will know happiness.

> **THE WORLD NEEDS YOUR VISION.**

Newsflash! If this card has come to you, you have a Vision.

Your ability to see a new reality can sometimes place you outside the accepted worldview and leave you feeling like there is something wrong with you. You do not fit in, and that is exactly why it would be good to share your version of what is possible. You are not simply out of step, you are ahead of the rest of us, and we need you to let us in on your vision. In our culture, we tend to ignore those ideas that we cannot see as clearly as you can.

This message is telling you to own your Vision, to express it in whatever ways you can, and to filter out the naysayers and the wet blankets. Above all, do not be discouraged if you do not receive the feedback and encouragement you desire. This is a time to cultivate faith in yourself and trust in your perceptions. Be patient with others who may be so entrenched in their worldview that they don't even know there are other possibilities.

The world needs your vision. Otherwise, why would you be having it? You yourself may have been the biggest dismisser of your unrealistic, impossible, and crazy vision. You get to have two out of the three: It's probably currently very unrealistic, and against this standard it is also totally crazy. That it may be impossible, at this point, does not matter. The most improbable things become possible when humanity's mindset shifts.

What matters is putting it out there. Be the caretaker of your vision. Help us see it. Others may just be ready to receive it. The time is right to believe in yourself.

> **THERE ARE ENOUGH TIME, MONEY, RESOURCES, AND LOVE FOR YOU.**

That about knocks down every argument you have for not being happy, doesn't it? So why aren't you finding this treasure trove of enough-ness? This message is letting you know that you are holding yourself back from receiving the abundance that is your birthright by the beliefs you hold and the actions you are taking (or not taking.) In short, you are creating the scarcity you are experiencing. To prove that you have enough time and money, log everything you spend and bring in, time- and money-wise, for at least a week. It won't take long before you see exactly where your time and money are going.

You may feel you don't have a choice about how you spend your resources, but you do. You could choose otherwise. Not that you would, but you could. The only meaningful gift is the one you are choosing to give, right?

Next, love yourself for who and where you are. Then demonstrate that love by plugging up your time, money, and resource drains. Stop overspending your money, time, and energy on activities (and people) that exhaust you. Start investing your time and energy into the dreams and goals you are neglecting.

There is enough if you are willing to ask it *of* yourself. As soon as you stop being stingy with you, the Universe will follow your lead. But you will have to change what you believe is possible. And you have to show the Universe you care enough about your dreams to actually work for them.

You may think you want it on a silver platter, but the Universe doesn't want to cheat you of the satisfaction of mastering the situation–with Its help.

> **THERE IS ENOUGH OF EVERYTHING YOU NEED TO FULFILL YOUR DREAMS.**

This is the Universe's best-kept secret. It is coming to you now as a reminder that there are no obstacles to fulfilling your dreams except the ones that you believe in.

Listen to how you speak of your dream: Could it happen, except that you lack the time, money, resources, connections, training, clarity, motivation, etc.? Do you wish for a magic wand? Dropping those beliefs is the first magical thing you can do. Simply identifying them is a powerful first step in disarming them.

How, exactly, do you think time, money, and other resources and tools are doled out? Answering this question will give you a good idea of where to look to uncover your limiting beliefs about how the world works.

The Universe wants you to know that no matter what you believe, there is enough, and you can fulfill your dreams. If you want to shift your sense of lack and limitation, look beneath the surface to see how fear prevents you from taking action to fulfill your dreams. Looking closer at your fear will uncover where you think the Universe has forgotten about you and is leaving you hanging.

In this life, the dance of creation has two partners, the Universe and you. Are you still dancing, or have you taken a seat on the sidelines? Be gentle with yourself, but know that when you are ready to get back into action, the Universe will be there to meet you, extending its hand with the tools, resources, and inspiration that you need.

> **Treat yourself with reverence.**
> **You are a wonderful mystery.**

You are an unlikely, unfathomable mystery of limitless potential. That means you can never be fully understood. There will always be a part of you that is unknown. Some things you cannot and will not ever understand.

Some people love mysteries. Others find them unsettling and annoying until they are solved. But you are a *wonderful* mystery, always about to reveal something unique and improbable, just by virtue of being alive and fully engaged.

You may have lost sight of what is so miraculous and special about you. Or you may be busily figuring it all out, waiting until after you've achieved your big goals to be impressed and to enjoy the process.

The Universe wants to remind you that this is a never-ending process. It is encouraging you to pause for a moment and reflect on this mysterious unfolding–the unending unfolding of you–and to adopt an attitude of reverence and awe for the whole experience. While you are observing your process, ask yourself if you are treating yourself with reverence, or simply squeezing out every last bit of energy in pursuit of your goals.

This message is about the process of shifting from having to know it all to enjoying making discoveries about yourself and your life. It is about adopting an attitude of openness and curiosity, acceptance and humility. It's okay to admit that you are making it up as you go along.

If you can't connect with treating yourself with reverence, perhaps you can ponder the mystery of what is yet to be, in the potential that you carry. What if your real reason for being here remained a mystery to you forever? Would life be any less sweet?

Trust your brilliance.

The Universe wants you to know that the definition of brilliant is "shining brightly, sparkling, glittering, lustrous."

Ask yourself: Isn't there a part of you–your eyes, your wit, your hands, your connection with children, your sewing creations, your love of gardening, the cards you send, your care of your pet, your delight in Dancing With the Stars, the hope you feel at your niece's graduation, your intense love, your very soul–that is brilliant?

There is a deep cultural, personal, psychological, and sociological prohibition against thinking of yourself as brilliant. It is more acceptable to deny your goodness and worthiness, as if that very denial makes you better and more worthy.

Perhaps lately you have been experiencing a fear of grandiosity and self-delusion if you think positively of yourself. No wonder you are all stuck and jumbled. There is a part of you that is lustrous and sparkling. To know that means simply to trust that it is so.

Why trust? Because each of us needs to possess a sense of core worthiness and beauty in order be a fully functioning person. Imagine the potential that could be unlocked if you started from a ground of worthiness instead of always feeling you need to become great before you can feel great and receive and do great things.

You know it is there. It's okay. You don't have to put it on a billboard. The truth is, each of us shines with the luster of something that is alive, unique, Universal, and beautiful. Your inner brilliance is both nothing special and very special. Claim it, trust it, live it. It is your source of power.

> **TRUST YOUR INTUITION. YOU ARE BRILLIANT.**

The word "brilliant" is a hang-up for you. Only specially qualified, singled-out, grade A people are brilliant, and you are not that. Maybe you were labeled brilliant and never felt you quite deserved it.

The truth is, we are all brilliant in our way. Brilliant simply means bright and shining. Your intuition is an inner guidance system that when followed sharpens and focuses your particular brilliance. It allows you to know and do things in perfect timing and to be at one with yourself.

It is time for you to slow down and listen to your intuition. Where does it want you to go? Or not go? The important thing to know is that the language of intuition is often not literal and the guidance not specific, at first. What may seem illogical and random can later be revealed as wise and well timed, even prescient. To follow your intuition means to be flexible enough to change your mind, shift direction, decline invitations, and at times speak up, all things you may have been trained not to do, because they are not "nice." You may have to wait until you have a clear answer from within before you can give one to someone else. This can make you appear to be evasive or insecure.

Don't let others' interpretations of your behavior prevent you from listening to your own guidance system.

The Universe wants you to know it is possible and fairly easy to respect your own needs and also be sensitive to the feelings of others. Nice isn't all it's cracked up to be, when the price is your own power to live the life that is right for you.

> **USE YOUR VOICE. YOU ARE SAFE AND STRONG.**

This is unusual advice, especially for you. What does it mean? "Use your voice" means just that. Say what's on your mind. How comfortable are you with singing? Asking for what you want? Saying what you know? Your voice is You.

To find your voice means to be equally comfortable with speaking and listening. You may be telling yourself you are a good listener, but are you really? You may be confusing good listening with letting others use you as a dumping ground for their "stuff."

You may have developed a protective reflex to stifle your own expression. It is time to undo that self-preservation instinct, because the threat is gone. This message is about liberation from self-imposed, or other-imposed quietness, rigidity, strictness, and codes of conduct. Not only is it okay to do that, it's essential. It's part of becoming who you are and sharing that with the world.

But before you can do that, you need to find out what is in there, all wild and raw. It is very liberating to step away from judgments and allow yourself to just tunelessly hum, vigorously warble, or whatever else is bubbling up from within.

Forget the critic. In fact, forget the whole audience! The only way to strengthen your voice is to use it. Get yourself a conversation partner. Start writing down your feelings and observations. Sing along with the radio. Write letters to the editor.

Find your voice, give yourself permission to use it, and you will find some personal power that you did not know you had.

> **WELCOME HOME TO YOURSELF, YOU PERFECT CREATURE.**

The Universe wants you to know that all of your seeking ultimately leads back to you. This is because you are a microcosm of the entire Universe.

If that feels too paradoxical to understand rationally, then think of it this way: You are a like a drop of water. Everything in you is exactly the same as everything found in all water. Learn about the drop of water and you know about water everywhere.

You are an extension and manifestation of divine creation. The Universe and you are made of the same stuff. This has vast implications for reality, divinity, time, meaning, and purpose.

It also means that all of the judgments and comparisons, the weighing and measuring of relative values lead exactly nowhere. The place to find the power and juice of Life is within. When you tap into your own power, you tap into Universal power. What's more, the more comfortable you get spending time with you and learning how to create your life, the more able you are to connect with that which is universal and common to all of life.

If you have been seeking outside yourself for answers, validation, or legitimacy, try looking within. You can trust what you find there, as long as you take the time to listen. The only way to know how something resonates with you is to become intimate with yourself. Make yourself at home in you, and you will never have to look for home "out there" again.

> **YOU ARE A BEAUTIFUL, PERFECT, AND WISE CREATOR.**

The Universe is asking you to get comfortable with thinking of yourself as someone who creates. We all create. We create conversations, goals, dreams, projects, cookies, decor, poems, music, relationships. That is what humans do, all day, every day.

It is time for you to have confidence not only in your ability to create but also in your worthiness to do it on purpose. It is okay to have a little more say in having the life you want to have. Try it. What would a beautiful, perfect, and wise creator do with the raw materials you have been given? It is time to start thinking like that, and seeing yourself as someone who, when working in alignment with Universal forces, can create a beautiful and perfect life.

You may be going through a time when it feels like life is happening to you, when circumstances are such that you would never purposefully choose to create. It is tempting to think of yourself as a victim when this happens. If you are feeling blindsided by life, the Universe wants to remind you that creating can be as simple as finding one personal choice you can make. Realize that there will always be things outside your control. So focus on what you can create, and by all means stay away from blame.

You can trace most of your life circumstances to choices and decisions you have made in your life. Some, of course, just happen. But only if you can resist the urge to be a victim of circumstance can you begin to understand that you have choices today, here and now. Hint: Look at the places where you feel you have no choice to see where the really powerful choices are.

YOU ARE A BEING OF LOVE AND BEAUTY.

You have been focusing on some areas of your personality or inner life that are less than satisfying to you. It is good to remember, in the midst of this hard work, that what you are doing is removing what is obscuring your essential goodness. You are not improving yourself. It is good to remember that this is who you are, not some unattainable ideal.

You must always strive to find and strengthen that essential core of love and beauty that is your essence, because that is where you are happy, fulfilled, content, and in your power.

If the word "power" gets in the way, just think of an orchid. Given the right conditions, is there anything that can keep it from blossoming? Is there anything that can blossom as that orchid in exactly that way? Being the orchid is its power. Key word: being.

Perhaps it is time to look at your environmental conditions and make sure they are the ideal ones for bringing forth your blossoms. Is the soil full of nutrients? Is the air clean and at the right temperature? Are you getting enough water? Tend to yourself as you would a precious flower. Find out what will make you blossom. Investigate what feeds your soul.

If you have been focusing on achievement, measuring your value by your doing, piling on chores, taking on more assignments, or simply feeling less-than, this message is here to remind you that what matters about you is not what you do but who you are.

YOU ARE A MIRACLE.

If you have been in a place of "so what?" this is message is urging you to stop taking yourself and existence for granted. What if each and every molecule of physical existence was invented purposefully, with a role to play in the whole?

What if you, exactly you, were a miracle of life, of creating, fighting disease, making new life, intelligent choice, whimsical activity, curiosity, reverence, seeking, and growth?

You can take for granted that you are alive, and you can downplay your role in the grand scheme, but at this moment you are invited to be present to the miracle of existence, and maybe even ask yourself, "How did I come to be?"

Spend some time going a little deeper into your personal philosophy of existence, and bring that depth into the rest of your day. Pondering mysteries is a great antidote to being weighed down with the particulars of everyday life.

Enjoy being you, for you are a miracle and sparkling. If you have lost your luster, it is important to spend some time getting in touch with how amazing you are, as a person and as a part of the vast creation, as much a little life-engine as every leaf and bumble bee.

You are a natural healer. Trust yourself.

Whether you make a mean batch of cookies, or know how to grow great African violets, love to shovel snow, are a good listener, or make things with your hands, connect with lots of people, or have a knack for bridging cultural differences, draw, sing, or write poetry, do nails or cut hair, you have a gift.

It may even be that you can ease physical pain and discomfort, or bring spiritual peace. This message comes to you now to encourage you to trust that what you have to offer is real, legitimate, and good. Something is making you hesitate to claim your gifts. Perhaps you are afraid of them when cast in the light of "healing."

Healing is nothing more than being the whole, congruent, real person inside and out that you are. When you trust yourself and take out the inner garbage, healing just happens. When you are in the healing mode, working to know yourself and to grow past your internally placed limitations, then you are a field of healing energy that benefits everyone who comes in contact with you.

In our culture, we have a tendency to equate power with material wealth and greatness with fame. This message is about resting in your own power quietly and feeling at home in you, exactly as you are, right now. It's about giving yourself credit for the healing you have already done and setting aside any need to inflate your ego either by grandiosity or false modesty.

You already know what to do and what not to do. Now it is time to share your healing gifts in the spirit of love. It is safe to trust yourself in this.

You are a wise healer.

Do you inwardly leap with hope when you get this message, because you have always suspected that you have the ability to heal? This message, then, is meant to encourage you to explore how to embody this truth in your life. If, on the other hand, you want to reject this message as blatantly false, then you have bought into the contemporary idea that only certain people have the ability to cause healing, and everybody else is less powerful than that.

The Universe wants you to know that all humans are healers. To heal, to embody the wholeness that we are is our entire life's work. By striving to live in a way that matches inside to outside, you heal. By having integrity, by loving and being loved, by living in your power, you heal. And when you heal, others heal, too.

The Universe is not a collection of separate particles that have a firm membrane around them, some in good shape while others are faulty. The Universe is of one fabric; when one part is affected, the whole is affected. To create a positive effect in the world, start with yourself. You are your own healer, first and foremost.

This message comes to you at a time when you are ready to appreciate, not your powers to cure, but your power to heal. You do this by cultivating trust in what you know from your senses and your perceptions, not only from books or authority figures. It takes inner strength to live by your own authority. If this all feels foreign and a little bit blasphemous to you, you have picked this message to begin exploring your concepts of power and authority, and quite possibly, to expand your idea of "God."

> **YOU ARE ALREADY WORTHY. THERE IS NOTHING TO EARN.**

Have you been obsessed with self-improvement?

There are two approaches to bettering yourself: for the joy of growth and the discovery of your human potential, or to improve upon a flawed and lacking self.

This message is gently reminding you that there is nothing about you that needs to be made up for, improved, or earned so that you can claim your seat at the feast of life. The same banquet is set for all of us. This means you do not have to do anything to have the same riches as everyone else. What are the riches? Loving relationships, personal fulfillment, a sense of meaning and purpose.

You are no better than or worse than anyone else. Some of your actions and choices may have caused you or others real pain and suffering. This puts you on the level with every other human being. You are free to improve, but remember, you already have an A. Now go and do some great work.

The Universe wants you to understand that in the mindset of comparing good versus bad there will always be pain. You may come up short today only to find that when you finally achieve that illusive goal and get into the right column, you still have a nagging feeling of not-enough-ness. Conversely, you may find that a great mistake actually contained some lopsided wisdom and has taken you to a place you needed to be for your healing.

Notice how much you keep score. Gently disengage from the either/ors and affirm that you are as worthy as everyone else. We are all here to learn something and become our best.

> **YOU ARE EXACTLY WHERE YOU ARE SUPPOSED TO BE. RELAX.**

There are no mistakes in the Universe. Do not bother asking about war and famine across the globe. Focus on you, right here, right now.

Wherever you are, be it comfortable, nerve-wracked, industrious, adrift, awkward, social, and cocooning–this is where you are supposed to be. Knock off criticizing yourself for where you are today. Also let go of worrying about down the road. ("If things continue like this...")

Try being a curious, sightseeing tourist in your own life, and find out everything you can about the landscape of being you right now. Are you feeling there is something that should definitely not be happening in your life today? Ask yourself, "What is the wisdom in this condition?" and "What do I need?" If you see that there is nothing significantly amiss to explain your persistent lack of contentment, ask yourself what thoughts or beliefs are dominating the inner landscape.

In either case, massive, sensible self-care might just be the order of the day. Until you get clarity, just do first things first. What's the most pressing need, and go from there. And keep it simple: sometimes the best thing to do is nothing.

On the Great Chess Board of Life, you have been plunked down exactly here. Let go of judgments and shame about where you are. Be kind and compassionate to yourself right now. In the process of accepting what is and tending to your basic needs, you might find that most of the problem evaporates when you befriend the moment instead of fighting it.

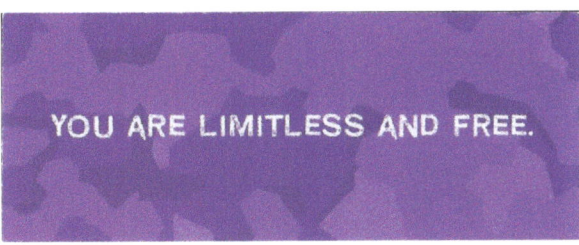

YOU ARE LIMITLESS AND FREE.

This message is about connecting with that part of us that cannot be defined at all and surely cannot be understood by our rational minds. It is a reminder that everything your life comprises today, your physical condition, your finances, where you live, what you "do," even your name and identity, are the short haul.

The long haul is the eternal you, the Soul, and it is much bigger. Limitless, in fact. And without a body, without time, without definition, and, without these temporal factors, free.

The Universe is reminding you that what you are now focused on is the smallest part of who you are. It wants you to focus on the Eternal. If you have lately found it a challenge to focus on the details, maybe your soul would like some timelessness. Timelessness can be found meandering without a watch or cell phone, listening to music lying down, meditating, becoming absorbed in making art, or watching the clouds.

If there is a specific issue you have been dealing with, this message can help you to shift focus and become larger than the problem for a moment. This might help you move through it with less pain. You do not have to be defined by anything. You can simply be in this moment, experiencing being alive without definition. That is true freedom. The human experience is deep enough to be simply experienced, without words.

The Universe invites you to take a deep breath, and notice that you are. The Universe is a very spacious place. Rest in that.

YOU ARE PERFECT. THERE IS NOTHING TO IMPROVE.

It is time to put away the self-improvement books! Take a deep breath. Relax. You are already okay. Yes, the Universe knows you are working through some things. One way to do that is with the mindset that you need to be fixed. The other way is with the awareness that you are on a journey of healing. One way comes from a place of being flawed, and the other speaks to potential. How could someone like you be already perfect? Perfection is a state of being. "Perfect" means whole and internally consistent. There are reasons and causes for everything you are working to correct and heal.

The trick is to find ways to allow the wholeness that you are to emerge from the circumstances that are calling your attention. The challenges you now face contain the seed of their own solution. In other words, how would an already whole person think, feel, and behave? Your circumstances will dictate how you answer that question. Whether you are working on prosperity issues, health issues, relationships, career or life purpose, try coming from that place of already-solved, and see how that changes your perceptions and behaviors.

Experiment with using less blaming and judging language to describe yourself or others in this situation. What if the way it is were exactly right? What if everything were exactly as it is supposed to be? What if you, exactly as you are right now, were worthy of love, receiving help, and about to blossom into another potential? Might you not begin to prepare for a birth, or a celebration, instead of railing against What Is? Don't miss the party! Instead, start getting ready. You are about to be born.

YOU ARE PRECIOUS AND BEAUTIFUL.

This message isn't only about beauty. It's about mirrors.

Have you ever had the experience of someone's face lighting up when you walk into the room? That expression of delight makes them beautiful, too. You become the mirror to each other, reflecting each other's preciousness.

When you have that experience, it can change the way you see yourself, enabling you to see through the eyes of love.

A mirror in your shoulder bag tells you that your face is okay, but this mirror, the mirror of human love, tells you that you are treasured, that you matter, that your mere presence brings delight and opens someone's heart. Perhaps also the Divine heart?

How can your heart not open in the presence of such love? And in this openhearted space, how much easier is it to see yourself as a serendipitous, happy, pleasing embodiment of Life itself. And when you see yourself that way, you become that.

Try it on today. This is the love that can transform the world. No person could hold herself in such esteem and not hold everything in creation in the same esteem, as the same Love.

It is time for you to see beauty and value in every circumstance and in every person, including yourself, if not in body and behavior, then in soul and spirit.

> **YOU ARE PRECIOUS AND UNIQUE.**
> **THERE IS NONE OTHER.**

Just think about that for a moment. Think of grains of sand, pebbles, shells, leaves, wildflowers, and snowflakes. When you examine them closely, you see that each one is unique. Once one is gone, it is gone forever.

The same is true of you. You can be categorized so many ways. You are a certain age, height, weight, eye color, gender. You are right- or left-handed, dyslexic, a skater, a mother, a friend, an employee. You are ranked and filed. You have numbers associated with your name. Yet none of it captures the uniqueness that is you. The way you see the world, what you notice, what you value. No one will ever perceive life the way you do, or love the way that you do. The instantaneous choices, the intentions, the fears and courage that guide you and create your life–no one else does any of those things exactly like you do.

It may be that you are someone who disappears in a gathering. You may look to others and listen rather than speak. You still have to listen to yourself. What is inside you is as valid as what others show on the outside.

You have been feeling less-than and comparing yourself to others around you who look like they have it all together. It takes courage to value yourself and to stop comparing yourself to others. The time is right for you to ask whether you fully appreciate all that goes into making you unique. The Universe wants you to know that somewhere there is a situation or person that needs exactly what you have to offer, and it's up to you to bring yourself fully into each moment so you can be found by what needs you. In being found, you find yourself, and then you are home.

YOU ARE THE SOUL OF GOODNESS.

Maybe you take for granted that you do good things for people, that you love and care for others, for creatures and for the earth. Maybe you have stopped noticing how your gratitude and appreciation create an elevated vibration around you, encouraging others to look for the good in any situation. Maybe you don't appreciate that you are there for others as a sounding board and guide, that you are trusted and trustworthy, wise, and helpful.

All your good instincts and actions, your thoughtfulness, and your humor help to make the world a better place for those around you. Your smile campaign? It's working. Your donations to worthy causes? They help. Your kind words, your volunteering, your sharing, all make a difference.

Your prayers are heard. Your heart radiates love. This vibration affects those who come into contact with you. People who need love can't help but be attracted to you. And when you are in your heart place, you cannot be depleted by giving of the love that you have cultivated through your own healing path.

The Universe is sending you this message to affirm that you are helping to shift consciousness through your loving intentions and actions. You already know that people around you are doing the best they can. With your influence, their potential for goodness is being awakened. You are a living embodiment of the quality of Goodness that exists as a force in the Universe. Your soul is here to express that goodness in the being that you are. Knowing this cannot harm you, for such is the nature of Goodness.

> **YOU DO ENOUGH. LET YOURSELF RECEIVE FROM THE LOVING UNIVERSE.**

That's right, you! Stop doing and just sit. Get yourself a cup of tea, get cozy, and relax. Breathe. Now, answer honestly: Do you have it set up that in order to receive the goodies in life, you have to work hard? You have created a situation in which you are indispensable (or want to believe that you are) and are in danger of overworking yourself to the point of exhaustion. It is essential that you do something to put yourself in an attitude of receptivity so that the Universe can refill your rapidly emptying stores of energy. Doing nothing is an excellent start. If you do not create the space for the Universe to support you, you will soon be running on empty.

If you have developed this way of living for fear that nobody knows or cares about you, remember that in order to receive you have to be willing to be the first to love you. Ask yourself how you can love yourself today. What self-care or spirit care activities have you let go by the wayside? When was the last time you did something just for yourself? What would you secretly love to do that nobody else on Earth would want or care about? A junky movie with butter-laden popcorn? A romance novel gulped down in one day? A facial? A hike in the woods or walk on the beach? A ride to an unknown destination? An afternoon with a blank notebook in a strange cafe?

If your heart leapt at one of those suggestions, stop right now and make a naughty but necessary list for yourself of what you will do to indulge yourself, then put it on your calendar. Prioritize you. Then see how the world looks once you have allowed yourself some refreshment.

YOU HAVE BRILLIANT IDEAS AND INSTINCTS.

The Universe wants you to know that brilliant isn't what you think it is. It is quieter and subtler than that. But brilliant is still bright, piercing, and alive.

Your wonderful mind is presenting you with the answers you need, and you are not paying attention. You may have gotten into the habit of demanding proof before you will give your ideas a chance to breathe. You may be talking yourself out of what you know, instead of trusting it and acting on it. You may not think you even *have* instincts.

Hint: Those who are seen as wise and brilliant have probably given their ideas a little more air and attention than the rest of us.

This message is a reminder to stop stopping yourself from doing what your instincts are telling you to do. Proof isn't needed right now. Give yourself credit for having a unique way of looking at things. You are partnering with the Force of Life to create the little corner of the Universe known as you. The Universe has given you the tools; it's your job to use them.

You can't know it all in advance in your head. Give yourself some momentum, and trust that you will know what to do once you get started.

It is suggested you share this message with a friend and take turns saying it to each other. ("You know, you have *brilliant* ideas and instincts!") If nothing else, it will teach you to recognize an idea or instinct when it shows up, and that is a very good first step toward strengthening your confidence and turning those ideas into something a little more than an idea.

> YOUR BEAUTY IS AN INSPIRATION TO OTHERS.

You didn't realize anyone noticed, did you? And you wouldn't call it beauty, right? Thank goodness there are others who see and appreciate you far more lovingly than you do yourself!

This message is meant to encourage you to see yourself as beautiful, and if necessary, to expand your concept of beauty. Look beyond the usual measures of beauty–symmetry, the perfect physique, or the one feature that stands out. See how your loving attitude, quirky take on life, supportiveness, and restless seeking, as well as your enormous feet and squinty eyes that miss nothing, create a perfectly consistent template that others find beautiful, like a poem, lived.

Then realize that what others see in you inspires them, not to be like you, but to be true to themselves, to be their own living poem.

If you still have doubts, find something beautiful in nature. Notice that for all its beauty, it also has flaws. If you look hard enough, you will find them. Then ask yourself what it is you focus on that allows you to see its beauty and not its flaws? Now apply that to yourself. It is all about focus, isn't it?

The Universe wants you to know that what others are focused on is your beauty, which feeds their inspiration. What is there to fear in seeing yourself that way and in being inspired by yourself? That is true empowerment, not the kind that leads to exaggerated self-importance, but the kind that allows you to build on your strengths and unlock more potential.

What a gift!

> **YOUR CREATIVITY IS DIVINELY DIRECTED. IT IS NOW SAFE TO CREATE.**

As a creative person, you have to master just one skill: creating–while your inner critic jumps up and down shouting in the background for you to stop.

The Universe wants you to know that you can deny your creative impulses only so long, and then you start to suffer energetic losses. You may be in such a state right now. This can be turned around in an instant by picking up the pen, the brush, the knitting needles or the measuring spoons, and getting busy.

Even before you pick up the implements of your craft, maybe your creative soul needs time to just waft about aimlessly. Maybe page through a book or take a stroll? Staring at clouds works, too. Your creativity is not self-indulgent, lazy, worthless, lightweight, insignificant, low class, unprofessional, or any of the other derogatory labels your inner critic can throw at you.

As a child of the Universe, you have all the credentials you need to step into the sandbox and play. This is not meant to demean what you do, or to downplay credentials, but to shift the emphasis from accomplishment to discovery, from finished product to creative process.

Focusing on those things that engender a sense of wonder will yield your most potent and satisfying results right now. Even if you have to hide your creative activity from everybody in your life because they happen to be wet blankets, do yourself a favor and stop trying to hide it from yourself. It is safe to create if you say it is. If you do it now, you will be nurtured in ways that you have been missing for a long time.

> **YOUR DREAMS AND INSPIRATIONS ARE DIVINELY DIRECTED.**

So don't ignore them, dismiss them, disrespect them, or scoff at them! Just honor them as something coming through you from Universal wisdom.

Magic happens when you honor a dream. It assumes a dignity and legitimacy that nurtures and helps you, in ways you could not have imagined. Forget the logical problem solving of your rational mind for now, and consider that your dreams and inspirations are the means by which your needs will be met.

What dreams are you entertaining? What have you been fantasizing about doing? What are the kernels of wisdom embedded in those fantasy scenarios? The key to knowing those answers is to get into actions that will allow the next steps to unfold.

Come to see your desires and inspirations as little gift tags, attached to invisible packages. It is up to you to take them in hand, and find the gifts they bring.

If you have developed the habit of ignoring your inner promptings, or if you do not allow yourself to be inspired, this message comes to you at a time when you are at risk of cutting off your lifeline to the Divine, which is, after all, the Source of everything.

You, too, are a vessel and messenger of Divine wisdom. Rather than looking for the hand to come down from the clouds, look within to the sparks of curiosity, the urgings of your heart, and the ideas that sparkle. There is your Divine communication.

> **Your inner wisdom is a Blessings Navigator. Follow it.**

What a radical idea! There is an inner compass that points to blessings. Isn't that kind of a dream come true?

Why, then, do you ignore those inner promptings? The simplest explanation is that by one means or another you have been taught to dismiss and distrust your own inner knowing.

We live in a culture that does not foster inner navigation. Adults are believed to know better than children, who are expected to follow someone else's timetable, fashion sense, sensory palette, ideas, and beliefs. It is no wonder that you have a hard time following your own instincts. You are completely out of practice.

If you picked this message, you may have begun experimenting with following your own compass. This starts with recognizing how it speaks to you. You may be a gut person or a heart person. You may hear a snippet of a song lyric that holds an important clue. You may feel you absolutely must turn here, or visit there, and have no idea why. Just practice following the prompts.

Then look for the blessings, gifts, and help that arrive. The Universe wants you to know that in everything from parking spots to business partners, your inner wisdom will help you find the blessings if you learn its language.

As you practice, and as your confidence grows, it will be easier to find your way to your own true north.

> **YOUR INSPIRATION AND HEART ARE WELCOME HERE.**

That is, what makes you happy inside and secretly smiling to yourself is welcome here in the rest of the world. We need that! The spark of Life that you embody is so welcome, dear one. We need your inspiration. We need your heart. They are your brilliance. It is okay to allow your sparkling, authentic jewel of a soul to shine.

It is okay, in fact, essential, for you to come out of the closet and share what makes your spirit sing and the creative impulses that are dancing to be expressed through you.

To be welcome means to be held in respectful expectation and loved. It means the door is open, come right in, make yourself at home. Be yourself. You can drop the act, drop the role, and just be you. It is not about fulfilling someone else's needs by being something different from who you are.

Not sure how to be you? Spend some time letting your creative soul follow what calls it. Give yourself long stretches of timelessness. Waste time, meander, dawdle, explore. Make nothing of it. Be curious. Let it go. Pick up tatters and collect them. Fall in love with a shadow. Be fascinated with things that cannot be expressed in words. Let yourself be inspired, innocent, and untamed.

Practice following your instincts when you are with others. Tell people how you feel, what you know, and what excites and inspires you. Share your crazy wisdom and secret knowing. Let people know what inspires you. Let people see that you are leading with your heart.

You have fallen in with other hearted ones, and it is safe now to be the poet that you are.

> **YOUR SONG IS A BEAUTIFUL INSPIRATION THAT TOUCHES MANY HEARTS.**

Your heart, most of all, is touched when you create. That is why you create, isn't it? This is the original creative instinct, to please ourselves. This is an excellent and valid place to start.

You have the heart and soul of a poet, and it needs to express the beauty that it feels. It is so much a part of who you are that you no longer see it as the rare and much needed gift to others that it is.

It is both difficult and easy to share this gift. This message comes to you to encourage you to consciously share. Be it an actual song, or something else you create that is equally harmonious and beautiful, it will touch many hearts.

An energy of love and beauty is transmitted to others when you share your creations. The more you share, the more love and beauty will flow.

If you have been telling yourself that it doesn't matter, or that nobody cares or receives your gift, you are not seeing the whole picture. In withholding or stifling your creative impulses, you are denying yourself and everyone else the heart benefits that your gifts bring.

If you are doubting that your art makes a difference, just ask yourself whether the world could use more–or less–beauty right now.

Go back to your muse and creative place, make it sacred again, and let your music flow!

YOUR SOUL IS AN INFALLIBLE GUIDE.

A part of you is still in Spirit. It is ephemeral, without body and beyond worldly affairs. It is not caught up in dilemmas and dramas. It is wise and peaceful, eternal, benevolent, abundant, and flowing.

A good way to tap into this part of yourself is to use the power of intention to connect with your deep soul wisdom. Simply state your intention to connect with soul guidance and allow a space within to open to receive. Suspend rational sense and allow yourself to hear what you hear, see what you see, feel what you feel, and know what you know. Hold an internal welcoming curiosity and let this part speak to you irrationally and foolishly. You can make sense of it later. Or you can let it remain the sacred poetry of your soul.

Connecting with the Eternal will give you a different perspective on your daily life. It will lift you out of your ordinary focus and help you see broader patterns and longer paths. And who knows? Maybe the irrational and the unlikely hold the key to solving some of your current problems.

You may begin to notice a tugging in your gut or heart. This is your Guide trying to direct you. Lightly experiment with following these promptings. A new flow will unfold; struggle and worry will abate. It is time for you to learn this skill, so that among other things, you can develop a deeper trust in life.

Your Soul knows what is best for you. It takes some practice, but after a while it will become easier to hear and to follow. And as you get better at this, you will come to understand that you can trust this wisdom always.

> **YOUR TIMING IS PERFECT. ALL IS WELL.**

Ah, time! It exists in ordinary reality but not in spirit.

This message comes to you now to remind you that there are Universal factors outside your awareness that are influencing how a situation is unfolding. The Universe wants you to know that in spirit there is no lateness, no rushing, no dawdling. All time and pace are divinely directed.

If you think of time as a stretchy band that lengthens and shortens, tightens and slackens, but is still of a piece, then you see that there is a flow that is malleable, orderly, and continuous. You may not be able to see the whole picture from where you stand, and you may feel impatient or afraid you are missing an opportunity.

Realize that wherever you are is exactly where you are supposed to be, so don't give up hope. Time is another way we are afraid the Universe is going to be stingy with us.

If you are resting, that is perfectly in time. If you are waiting, that is okay, too. You may need more clarity. If you are full speed ahead, then, perfect! Whenever you "arrive" at whatever pace, as dictated by your wisdom and the Universal forces cooperating with you, is the perfect timing for you.

Don't let other people impose their timing–or their ideas about your timing–on you. There is a time and place for following clock time and calendars, and a time to follow your own rhythms. Finding that balance gives you choice and power in this situation and in the whole of life.

YOUR UNIQUE GIFTS ARE WELCOME AND NEEDED AT THIS TIME.

Now is the time you have been waiting for, preparing for, and working toward. Now is the time, within and without, to bring your gifts to the fore and share them with the world.

Whatever way you have been thinking of doing this is the right way to do it. It does not matter the scale. You can share with one person or the whole world. It's your choice.

It is time to stop hoarding your talents, your great ideas, your willingness, your sense of humor, or whatever it is that you are good at. You may have been telling yourself that your gifts are dumb, stupid, and not real. Stop that right now!

If you want to bag groceries and are good at it, do that!

If you want to write and produce a play, do that!

Got a knack for baking, knitting, organizing, or rubbing backs? Whatever it is, it is no more than a vehicle for getting you out into the world, connecting with others, and being part of the great human party. It will evolve from there, but you have to start with the impulse. Once you follow it, you give the green light to your being that says, "I'm listening! What's next?"

You may have bought into the idea that anybody can do what you can do, or that being a (fill in the blank) is no big deal. The point is, you are unique, and your unique vibrational pattern is what makes what you do and how you do it special.

You will make a positive difference in the lives of others and feel better about your life if you share the wealth and give of yourself.

Where To Go From Here

If you, like I, reach the end of a book and feel a tug of sorrow, take a moment and breathe into that sorrow. Honor it, for it represents a heart that is alive. Endings are everywhere. We don't often stop to honor them. Bless you for loving yourself and life that much.

I want to offer you some suggestions for where to go from here, the end of the book. First, keep going back to the book. Have you ever had the feeling that new words and ideas had snuck into a book after you thought you'd read the whole thing? Well, I did revise it, but so have you revised you. You've grown since you began. You can always go back and see what you might have missed the first time.

Here's an even more fun suggestion: Make your own Soul Message cards. Listen in to your own heart and wisdom for the messages you or your friends most need to hear. What messages would be powerful antidotes to the ones that are causing suffering? You can even use world events to inspire you. What are the beliefs that lead to the choices some people make? Create a healing message for those beliefs. You will help heal the world.

Make a Soul Message journal. Each day you pick a message, write about what it means for you, what it touched, the revolution that it started. Or maybe it was a quiet but sure confirmation that you are on the right path. Don't confine your journal to writing if you don't want to. Draw, cut and paste things into it. Let your creative soul have fun.

Create affirmations from the Soul Messages. Affirmations are I-messages. Soul Messages are ah-messages. They can wash over your soul, giving you the experience of receiving good news about who you are and how the Universe works. I-messages can become your own tool for reinforcing those truths and empowering you to live the new reality you intend to create.

For example, The World Is Blessed That You Are Here becomes "The world is blessed that I am here." You can also create variations: "My presence is a blessing to all whom I meet today." "I am fully present in each moment." "I easily bring my gifts out into the world." Keep going until you've said it all. Then write them down, type them up, print them out, read them aloud, record them and listen, all of the above, or something else.

My favorite thing to do with affirmations is to write a manifesto full of empowering, inspiring ideas that directly counter the limiting ones I am healing, and print it out and post it on the wall that I look at when I look up from my writing. You can also write them on cards and place them strategically around your home, or use them as bookmarks.

Share the Soul Messages. From my website you can download a file that you can print out and cut up yourself, the ultra quick and inexpensive way to get a new set of cards. My website will also tell you where you can buy a set of printed cards. Soul Messages make lovely gifts for best friends, beloved family members, clients, therapists, sponsees, sponsors, and you can use them for raffles and door prizes. You can buy an extra set to give away, one card at a time, as gift enclosures or serendipitous secret love notes.

Share your Soul Messages journey with me and others by visiting my website (www.phylliscapanna.com) or the Soul Messages Facebook page (www.facebook.com/lavishlovenotesforthesoul). I LOVE hearing from you!

You are precious and wonderful!

Other Titles by Phyllis Capanna

To Whom It May Concern: Prayers Without the G-Word, a collection of prayers and poems addressing the Divine in many ways, providing inspiration for spiritual seekers whose journey takes them off the beaten path. Reflecting the author's personal roadmap for connecting with That Which Is, the poems speak to the rewards of the road, as well as the joys of reaching a destination.

Stay Connected

I want to thank you for reading this book and invite you to stay connected:

To join my mailing list, receive updates, news of my physical world whereabouts, advance publication notice, and to read my blog, The Joy Report, visit www.phylliscapanna.com.

Please consider writing a review of Soul Messages on Amazon or another online retailer where you buy books. Reviews help me get found by search engines and increase book sales, which help to keep me off the streets and out of unsuspecting employers' offices and agencies, where unhappy writers have been known to create havoc and adversely affect the entire economy of the world. Therefore, reviews promote world peace and economic stability. Thanks for doing your part.

www.ingramcontent.com/pod-product-compliance
Lightning Source LLC
LaVergne TN
LVHW010030070426
835512LV00004B/51